I0815553

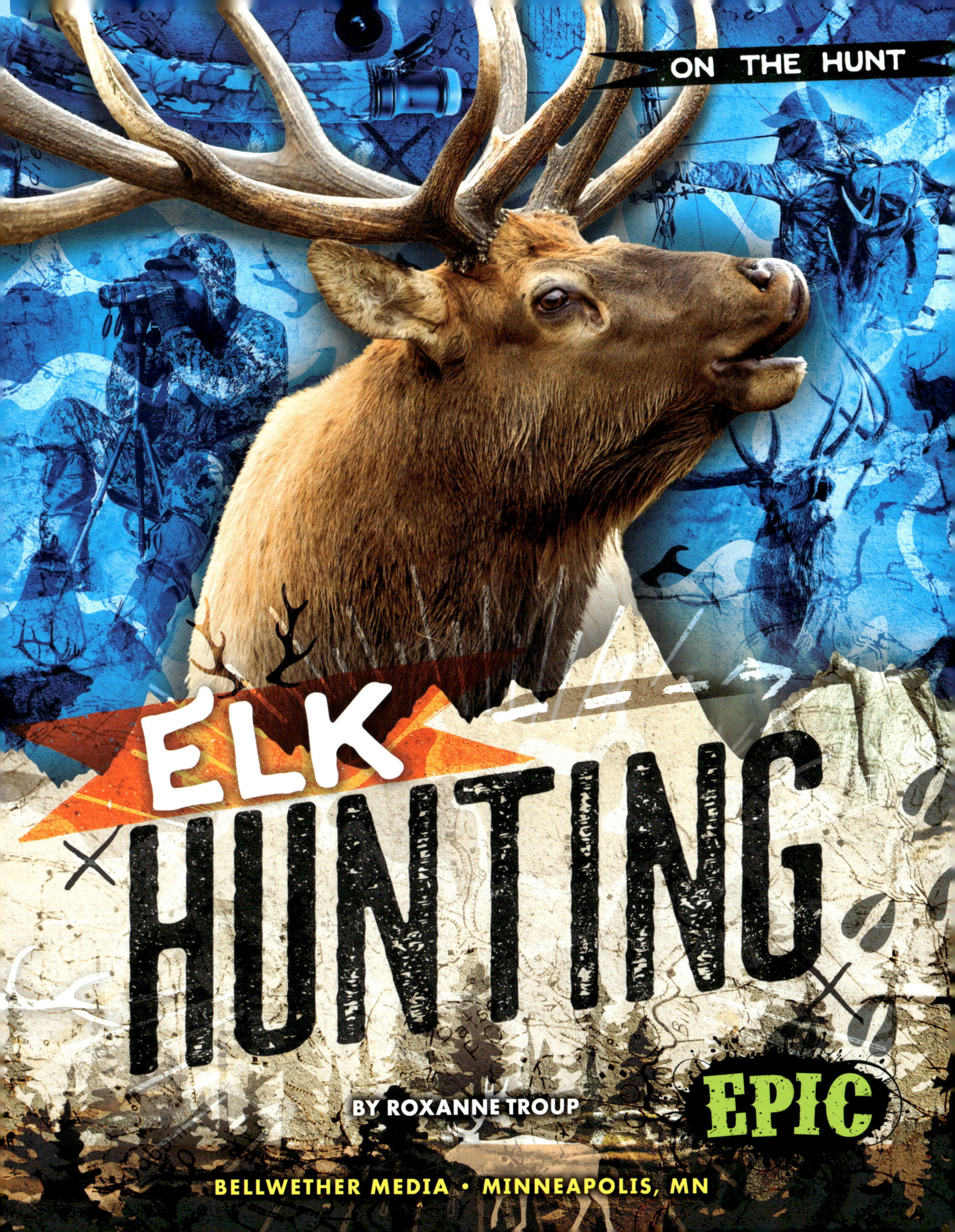
ON THE HUNT
ELK
HUNTING
BY ROXANNE TROUP
EPIC
BELLWETHER MEDIA • MINNEAPOLIS, MN

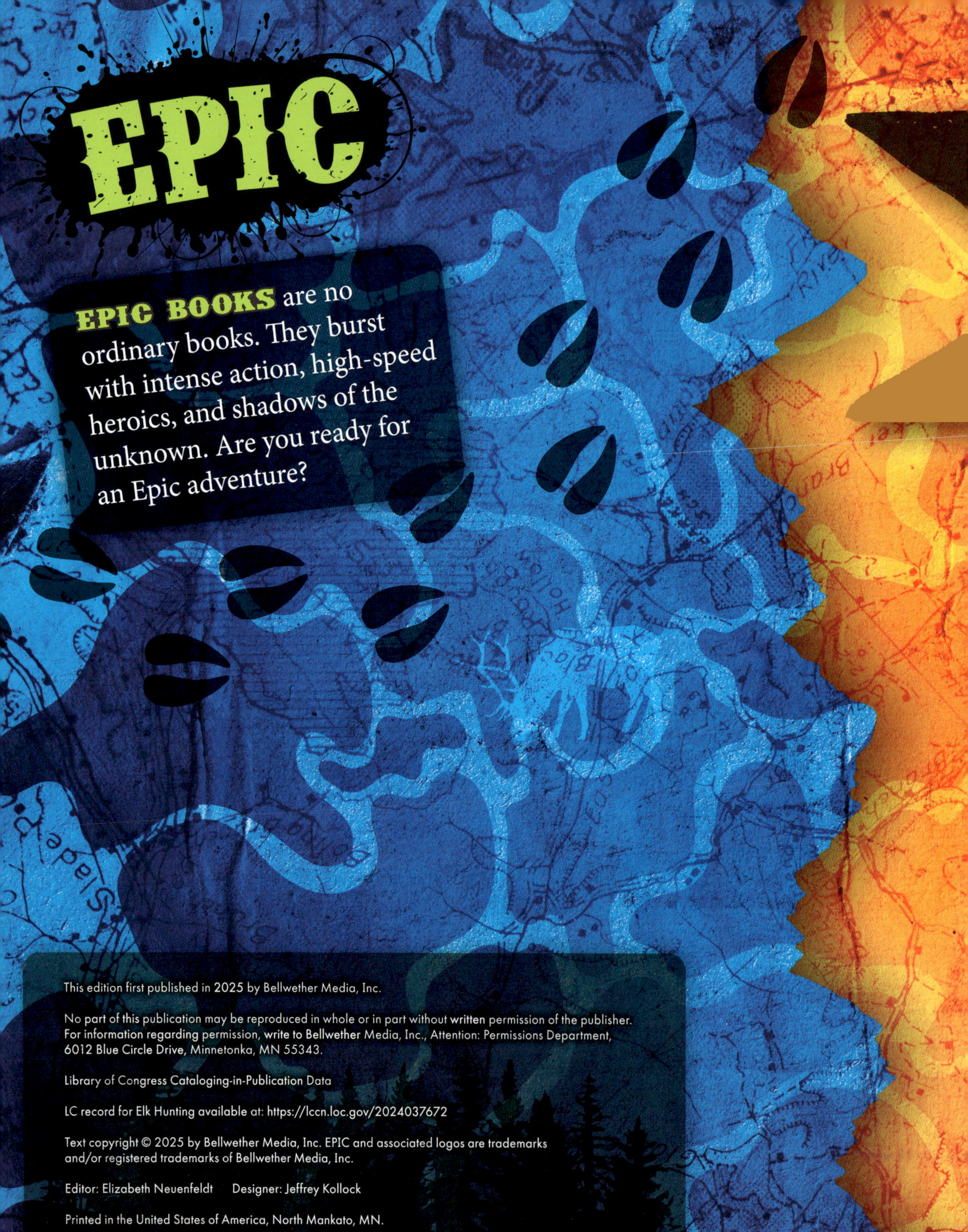

EPIC BOOKS are no ordinary books. They burst with intense action, high-speed heroics, and shadows of the unknown. Are you ready for an Epic adventure?

This edition first published in 2025 by Bellwether Media, Inc.

Library of Congress Cataloging-in-Publication Data

LC record for Elk Hunting available at: https://lccn.loc.gov/2024037672

Editor: Elizabeth Neuenfeldt Designer: Jeffrey Kollock

Printed in the United States of America, North Mankato, MN.

TABLE OF CONTENTS

WILDERNESS HUNT

The gear is packed. The truck is loaded. Two hunters drive into the mountains.

They make camp before hiking into the forest. Will they see any elk today?

WHAT IS ELK HUNTING?

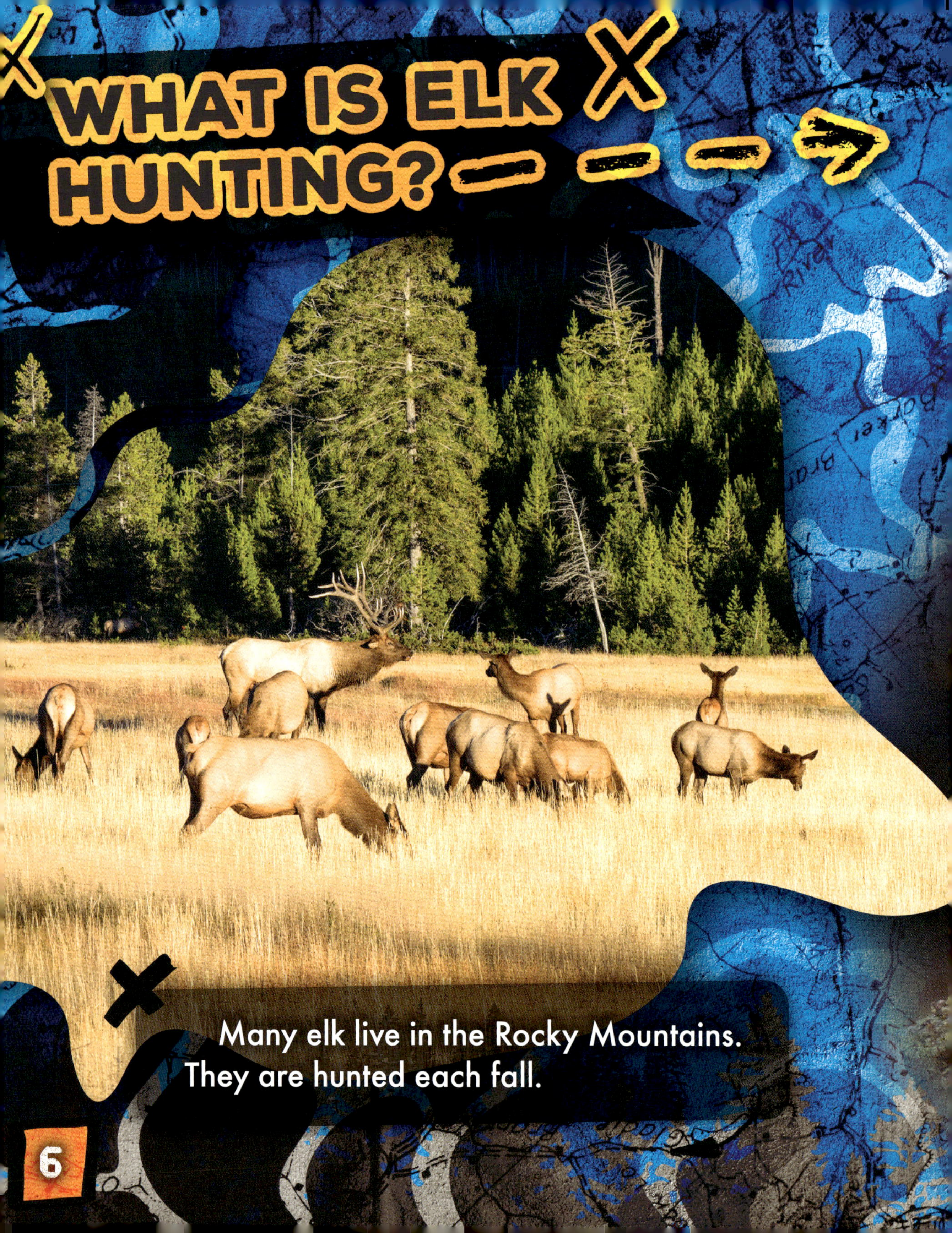

Many elk live in the Rocky Mountains. They are hunted each fall.

Fall is the time elk **rut**. They call to each other. This makes it easier for hunters to find elk.

Elk have a large **range**. They can be hard to hunt. Hunters must be in good shape.

Elk hunters camp outdoors. They track elk. Hunters may use **blinds** or **tree stands**.

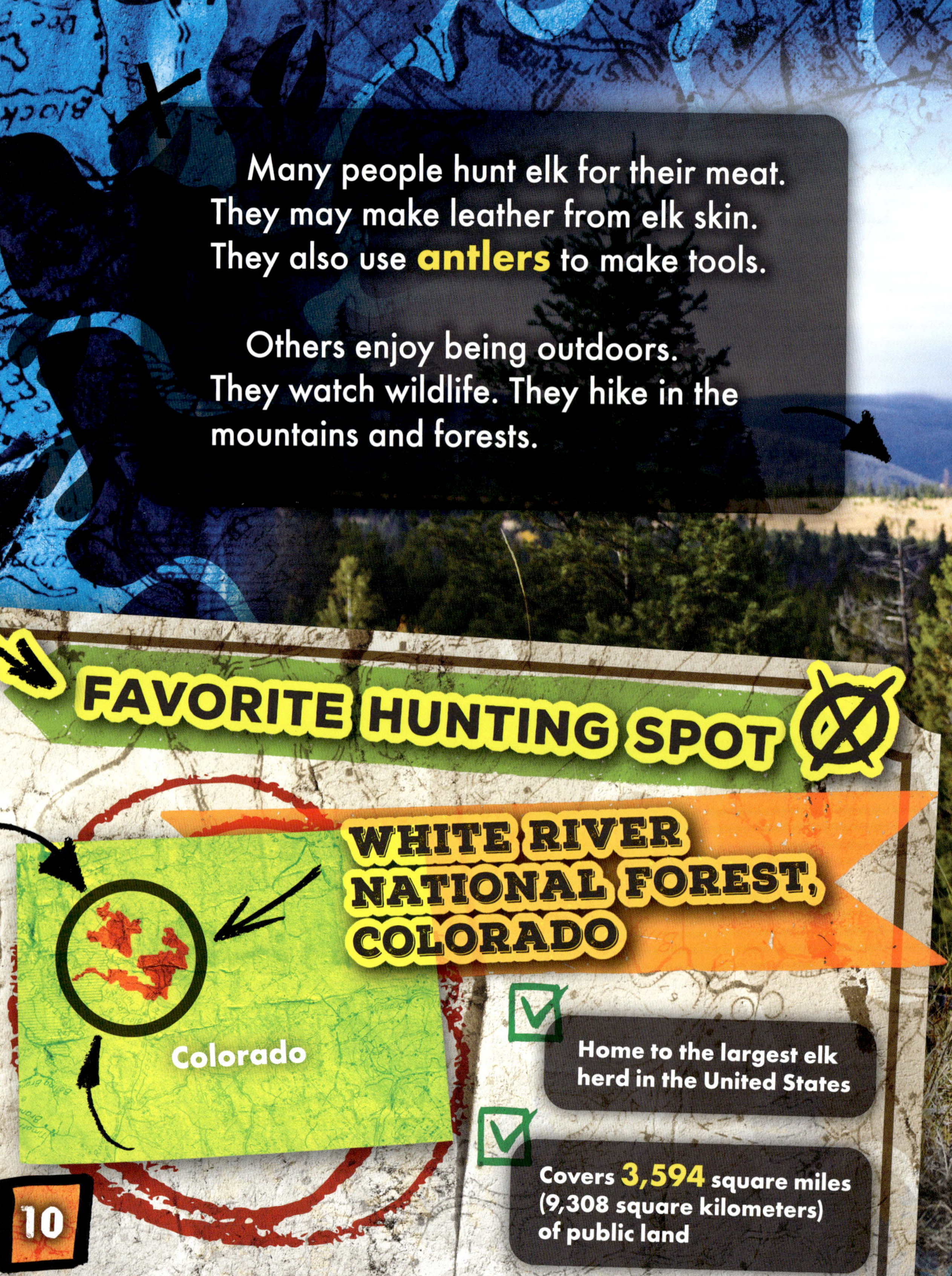

Many people hunt elk for their meat. They may make leather from elk skin. They also use **antlers** to make tools.

Others enjoy being outdoors. They watch wildlife. They hike in the mountains and forests.

FAVORITE HUNTING SPOT

WHITE RIVER NATIONAL FOREST, COLORADO

- Home to the largest elk herd in the United States
- Covers **3,594** square miles (9,308 square kilometers) of public land

antlers

PLANNING TO HUNT

Hunters spend many days on an elk hunt. They need more than a rifle or a bow.

They bring food, water, and camping gear. They also need extra clothes and **emergency supplies**. Maps and **GPS** devices keep hunters from getting lost.

Elk can be hard to find. Some hunters **bugle** to draw elk close.

BUGLE TIME

Elk often bugle after sunset and before sunrise. They also bugle at night.

This sound can be heard from far away.

Elk can sense nearby humans. Hunters must spot their targets from far away. Hunters use binoculars and a **rangefinder**.

Hunters stay very quiet.
They wear **camouflage**.

SAFE FOR EVERYONE

Hunters must have a **license** to hunt elk. But not every state offers them. States also limit the number of licenses sold each fall.

This keeps the number of elk from getting too low.

LUCK OF THE DRAW

Some states hold drawings for elk licenses. People interested in hunting apply for a license each year. If their name is drawn, they can buy it!

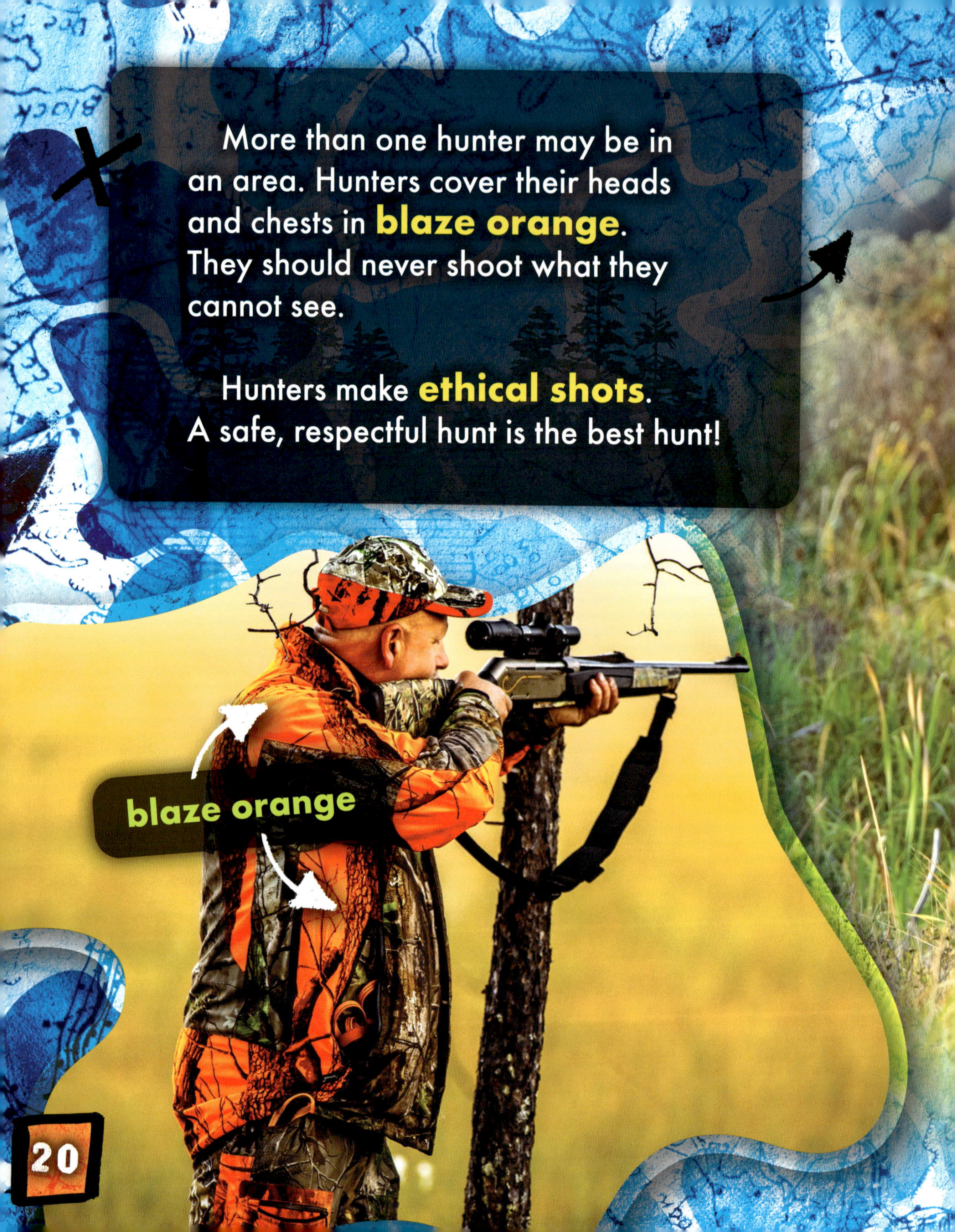

More than one hunter may be in an area. Hunters cover their heads and chests in **blaze orange**. They should never shoot what they cannot see.

Hunters make **ethical shots**. A safe, respectful hunt is the best hunt!

ethical shot placement

GLOSSARY

antlers—branched bones on the heads of some animals

blaze orange—a bright orange color that hunters wear for safety

blinds—small huts or closed spaces in which hunters wait

bugle—to make a male elk call

camouflage—a fabric that uses colors and patterns to blend in with surroundings

emergency supplies—supplies used during a sudden, dangerous event

ethical shots—clean shots that reduce pain and suffering to animals

GPS—global positioning system; GPS is a system people use to find locations.

license—a document that gives hunters legal permission to harvest a certain type of animal

range—the area where an animal can be found

rangefinder—a camera-like device that measures distance

rut—look for mates; mates are two animals that join together to make young.

tree stands—raised platforms on which hunters wait and watch for elk

TO LEARN MORE

AT THE LIBRARY

Conley, Kate. *The Hunting Encyclopedia.* Minneapolis, Minn.: Abdo Reference, 2024.

Roe, Monica. *Elk Hunt Adventure.* North Mankato, Minn.: Capstone, 2022.

Troup, Roxanne. *Deer Hunting.* Minneapolis, Minn.: Bellwether Media, 2025.

ON THE WEB

FACTSURFER

Factsurfer.com gives you a safe, fun way to find more information.

1. Go to www.factsurfer.com.
2. Enter "elk hunting" into the search box and click 🔍.
3. Select your book cover to see a list of related content.

INDEX

The images in this book are reproduced through the courtesy of: Tom Tietz, cover, p. 6; Harry Collins Photography, pp. 3, 7 (range); Cavan Images/ Alamy, pp. 4, 8, 12; Martina Birnbaum, p. 5; Thomas Torget, p. 7; Kolton Bachman, p. 9; T-I, p. 9 (blind); OUTDOOR_MEDIA, p. 11; B Norris, p. 11 (antlers); melissamn, p. 13; Jeffrey B. Banke, p. 13 (bow); Guy J. Sagi, p. 13 (rifle); Kazu8, p. 13 (camping gear); Alex Kosev, p. 13 (emergency supplies); Stocksnapper, p. 13 (GPS device); Nathan Allred/ Alamy, p. 14; Aline Bedard, p. 15; ZoranOrcik, p. 16; muroPhotographer, p. 16 (rangefinder); Neil Podoll, p. 17; Rodneymac, p. 18; R K Sewell Photography, p. 19; Robert Nyholm, p. 20; Jack Bell Photography, p. 21; MyImages - Micha, p. 23.